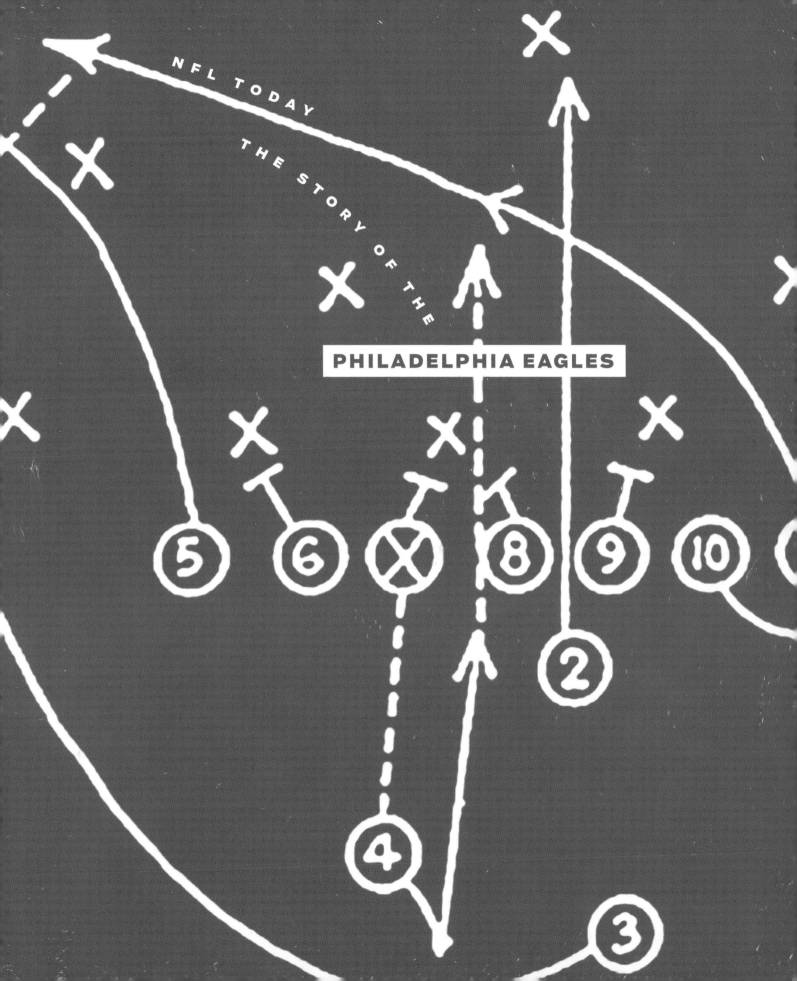

NFL TODAY

THE STORY OF THE

PHILADELPHIA EAGLES

NFL TODAY

THE STORY OF THE PHILADELPHIA EAGLES

NATE FRISCH

CREATIVE EDUCATION

PUBLISHED BY CREATIVE EDUCATION
P.O. BOX 227, MANKATO, MINNESOTA 56002
CREATIVE EDUCATION IS AN IMPRINT OF THE CREATIVE COMPANY
WWW.THECREATIVECOMPANY.US

DESIGN AND PRODUCTION BY BLUE DESIGN
ART DIRECTION BY RITA MARSHALL
PRINTED IN THE UNITED STATES OF AMERICA

PHOTOGRAPHS BY AP IMAGES, CORBIS (BETTMANN, RICHARD CUMMINS), GETTY IMAGES (JEFF CURRY, JONATHAN DANIEL/ALLSPORT, JERRY DRIENDL, STEPHEN DUNN, FOCUS ON SPORT, CHRIS GARDNER, DREW HALLOWELL, DREW HALLOWELL/PHILADELPHIA EAGLES, HARRY HOW, KIDWILER COLLECTION/ DIAMOND IMAGES, HAROLD M. LAMBERT/LAMBERT, KIRBY LEE/NFL, HUNTER MARTIN, HUNTER MARTIN/NFL, HUNTER MARTIN/PHILADELPHIA EAGLES, PATRICK MCDERMOTT, JOHN MCDONNELL/ WASHINGTON POST, AL MESSERSCHMIDT, RONALD C. MODRA/SPORTS IMAGERY, NFL, DOUG PENSINGER, ROBERT RIGER, ELIOT J. SCHECHTER, VIC STEIN/NFL)

COPYRIGHT © 2014 CREATIVE EDUCATION

LIBRARY OF CONGRESS CATALOGING-IN-PUBLICATION DATA
FRISCH, NATE.
THE STORY OF THE PHILADELPHIA EAGLES / BY NATE FRISCH.
P. CM. — (NFL TODAY)
INCLUDES INDEX.
SUMMARY: THE HISTORY OF THE NATIONAL FOOTBALL LEAGUE'S PHILADELPHIA EAGLES, SURVEYING THE FRANCHISE'S BIGGEST STARS AND MOST MEMORABLE MOMENTS FROM ITS INAUGURAL SEASON IN 1924 TO TODAY.
ISBN 978-1-60818-315-9
1. PHILADELPHIA EAGLES (FOOTBALL TEAM)—HISTORY—JUVENILE LITERATURE. I. TITLE.

GV956.P44F75 2013
796.332'640974811—DC23   2012033814

FIRST EDITION
9 8 7 6 5 4 3 2 1

COVER: RUNNING BACK LeSEAN McCOY
PAGE 2: END JASON BABIN
PAGES 4–5: 1962 EAGLES DEFENSE
PAGE 6: FREE SAFETY BRIAN DAWKINS

TABLE OF CONTENTS

PHILADELPHIA IS KNOWN AS THE "CITY OF BROTHERLY LOVE"

The Eagles Take Flight

In many respects, Philadelphia, Pennsylvania, was the birthplace of America and American ideals. It was here that the Declaration of Independence and the United States Constitution were signed. During the Revolutionary War fought to gain freedom from Great Britain, Philadelphia served as a center for military strategy. The largest city in Pennsylvania also served a stint as the capital of the nation in the late 1700s, and today it is recognized for its rich history and such iconic sights as Independence Hall and the Liberty Bell.

Philadelphia also has a rich football history, and a professional team known as the Yellow Jackets began playing there around the turn of the 20th century. Based out of Frankford—a northeastern section of Philadelphia—the Yellow Jackets competed independently until 1924, when the franchise joined the National Football League (NFL). In 1931, the Frankford Yellow Jackets went bankrupt and folded. Two years later, the franchise was given new life when Bert Bell and Lud Wray—both former football players—bought the team. They renamed the club the Eagles—birds symbolic of

A SNOWSTORM COULDN'T STOP THE EAGLES FROM WINNING THE 1948 TITLE

Earle "Greasy" Neale

COACH / EAGLES SEASONS: 1941–50

If a team is only as good as the man leading it, then Earle "Greasy" Neale—who kept his team at the top of its game for nearly a decade—is surely one of the best coaches in Eagles history. Neale led the Eagles to three straight Eastern Division crowns from 1947 to 1949 and two NFL championships in 1948 and 1949. The back-to-back championships were won in shutouts, a feat that still has not been duplicated by any other team. Neale loved to study game film, and his observations helped him produce many innovative ideas that remain a part of the game today. Neale's most important innovation, however, was the "Eagle Defense," which later evolved into the "4-3" defense (four linemen and three linebackers) that is still common in today's game. Before he gained renown as a football coach, Neale earned a measure of success in professional baseball as a young man. He played outfield for the Cincinnati Reds and hit for a .357 average during the 1919 World Series against the Chicago White Sox.

"A team is only as good as the man leading it."

American freedom and a fitting mascot for the city of Philadelphia.

It took time, however, for the fledgling Eagles to take flight. In fact, they would play for a decade before recording a winning season. The NFL was very different in those days. Until Bell proposed in 1935 that the NFL hold a draft to evenly distribute college players among all teams, whichever teams could pay the most and attract the best players had a major advantage. Professional football was not yet an especially profitable career, and college stars, even when drafted, often decided not to play in the NFL. Until the league mandated the use of helmets in 1939, players such as Philadelphia's tough (or foolish) Bill Hewitt—who played both offensive and defensive end—refused to wear them. In that era, players tended to be much smaller than players today, and many played multiple positions. In 1939, the Eagles drafted 5-foot-7 Davey O'Brien, who turned out to be one of Philadelphia's first stars while playing as quarterback, defensive back, and punter.

In 1941, wealthy steel businessman Alexis Thompson purchased the struggling Eagles. Thompson immediately hired Earle "Greasy" Neale as Philadelphia's coach. Neale had a long track record of success as a college coach and had led Washington & Jefferson College to the 1922 Rose Bowl. With Neale's hiring, Thompson was confident his franchise had taken its first big step in the right direction.

As young men went overseas to fight in World War II in the early 1940s, the NFL struggled with a shortage of players. To field a team, the Eagles formed a temporary merger with the cross-state Pittsburgh Steelers in 1943. The "Steagles" proved to be a formidable team, posting a 5–4–1 record, the first winning season for Philadelphia. But after just one season, the Phil-Pitt merger was dissolved, and Philadelphia had its own team back.

In 1944, the Eagles drafted the second part of their championship formula: running back Steve Van Buren. Playing alongside quarterback Tommy Thompson and (starting in 1947) two-way end Pete Pihos,

"There were none greater."

**ALEX WOJCIECHOWICZ
ON GREASY NEALE**

Van Buren quickly gave Philadelphia one of the most feared offenses in the league. The Eagles soared up the standings, finishing 1944 with a 7–1–2 record.

In 1947, Philadelphia finally claimed its first Eastern Division title. The Eagles fell a touchdown short to the Chicago Cardinals in the 1947 NFL Championship Game, but they came back in 1948 hungrier than ever. After going 9–2–1, the Eagles found themselves in a rematch with Chicago for the NFL title. On an almost unplayable, snow-covered field in Philadelphia's Shibe Park, the game went scoreless until the fourth quarter, when Van Buren powered into the end zone for the game's only touchdown and the Eagles' first NFL championship.

 he next season, Coach Neale led the Eagles to an 11–1 mark and a return to the NFL Championship Game. Playing this time on the mud-soaked field of the Los Angeles Memorial Coliseum, Van Buren set an NFL playoff record with 196 rushing yards as the Eagles blanked the Los Angeles Rams 14–0. Van Buren was the hero again, but the Eagles players gave much of the credit to Neale. "Most of the success of the Eagles must go to Greasy Neale," Eagles linebacker and center Alex Wojciechowicz later said. "Of my 13 years in the league, there were none greater. He was a fine teacher and leader."

The heart of the Philadelphia teams of the '50s was Chuck Bednarik. After being drafted by the Eagles in 1949, the former University of Pennsylvania All-American made an immediate impact, starting at linebacker on Philadelphia's 1949 championship team. The Eagles quickly realized that Bednarik was too valuable to waste on the sidelines and made him—like Wojciechowicz before him—the starting center as well. So rarely did Bednarik come out of games that he became known as the "60-Minute Man." Playing through torn tendons and broken bones, Bednarik would miss only 3 games in 14 NFL seasons.

Although the Eagles did not excel as a team for much of the 1950s, they did treat fans to some impressive individual performances. In 1953, quarterbacks Bobby Thomason and Adrian Burk combined to pass for a league-high 3,250 yards, while Pihos led the league with 1,049 receiving yards and 10

Football on the Small Screen

Professional football has enjoyed remarkable popularity among the American public, a fact that can be largely attributed to its relationship with television. Fast-paced and exciting, the NFL's high level of football is perfect for the small screen, and it all started on October 22, 1939, when the Philadelphia Eagles played in the first televised NFL game. In front of 13,050 fans at Ebbets Field in New York, the Eagles matched up against Brooklyn's Dodgers and their star quarterback, Ace Parker. The NBC network broadcast the game to approximately 500 television sets in the New York area and held a special viewing of the game at the site of New York's World's Fair. The broadcast didn't have any commercials to interrupt the action, but the early broadcast equipment periodically lost picture when cloud cover blocked out the light that the cameras needed. When the screen would go blank, the broadcast team would simply revert to a radio broadcast until the clouds passed and there was adequate light again. The Eagles lost the game 23–14 but earned a special place in NFL broadcasting history.

WATCHING FOOTBALL ON TELEVISION HAS BEEN A POPULAR PASTIME FOR DECADES

CHUCK BEDNARIK DELIVERED BONE-CRUSHING TACKLES NEARLY EVERY GAME

OPPOSING DEFENSES HAD TROUBLE COVERING ALL-PRO STAR PETE PIHOS

touchdowns. The next year, wide receiver and placekicker Bobby Walston topped the league in scoring with 114 points.

I n 1958, the team moved from Shibe Park (which had been renamed Connie Mack Stadium in 1953) to the larger University of Pennsylvania's Franklin Field, enabling their fan attendance to nearly double. That year, Bednarik suffered a knee injury that robbed him of the mobility needed to play linebacker. Yet he inspired talented teammates such as running back Tommy McDonald and receiver Pete Retzlaff by continuing to snap the ball on offense. It was this type of toughness that helped keep the team respectable during the playoff drought of the '50s.

Steve Van Buren

RUNNING BACK / EAGLES SEASONS: 1944–51 / HEIGHT: 6 FEET / WEIGHT: 200 POUNDS

Before the Eagles selected Steve Van Buren with the fifth overall pick in the 1944 NFL Draft, the team had never finished above third place in its division. Van Buren immediately took his place as one of the best athletes in the NFL and soon led Philadelphia to three consecutive division titles and two NFL championships. In 1945, Van Buren earned a remarkable "triple crown" by leading the league in rushing yards, points scored, and kickoff return yards. He excelled by using a relentless running style that wore down opposing defenses and created running holes where there were none. One of his most memorable performances came in the 1949 NFL Championship Game, when he carried the ball 31 times for 196 yards in the Eagles' 14–0 victory over the Los Angeles Rams. "They were the glamour boys of the NFL. They were a great team," Eagles linebacker and center Chuck Bednarik said of the Rams. "But he just put us on his shoulders and absolutely ran wild on that day." When Van Buren retired in 1951, he was the NFL's all-time leading rusher with a total of 5,860 yards.

Champions Again

Led by quarterback Norm Van Brocklin and "60-Minute Man" Chuck Bednarik, the 1960 Eagles fought their way to the NFL Championship Game for the third time in 13 seasons. The game was played at the Eagles' home venue, Franklin Field, against the Western Division champion Green Bay Packers. After legendary quarterback Bart Starr and his fellow Packers took an early lead with 2 field goals, the Eagles put 10 points on the board before the half. After a scoreless third quarter, the Packers took a 13–10 lead early in the fourth quarter. Eagles running back Ted Dean then took matters into his own hands, returning the ensuing kickoff deep into Packers territory and shortly thereafter running the ball into the end zone to give Philadelphia the lead again. The Packers launched one last drive, but Bednarik stepped up to stop running back Jim Taylor on the Eagles' eight-yard line as the clock ran out. The champion Eagles had handed Packers coach Vince Lombardi his only career playoff loss. "The tackle I made on Taylor was the greatest play I ever made," Bednarik later said.

CHUCK BEDNARIK AND NORM VAN BROCKLIN CELEBRATED WITH COACH BUCK SHAW (CENTER)

Philadelphia Legends

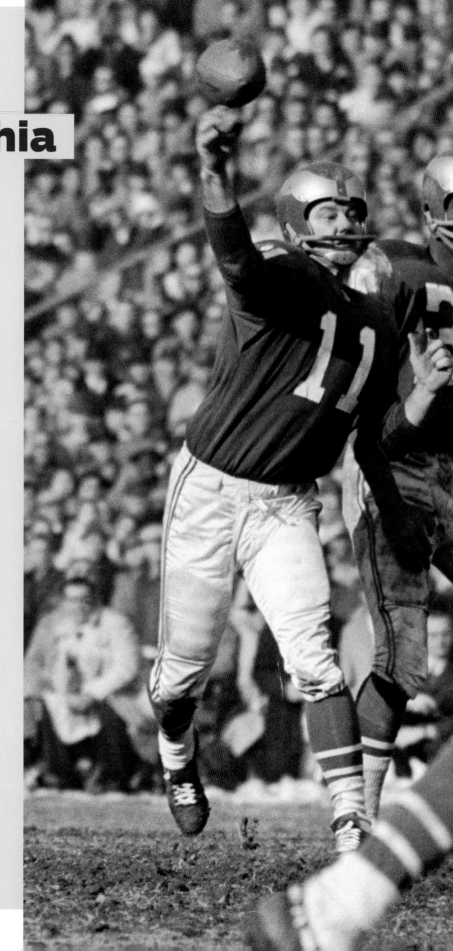

In 1958, Philadelphia brought in another player who would eventually be enshrined in the Pro Football Hall of Fame: former Los Angeles Rams quarterback Norm "The Dutchman" Van Brocklin. Although the Eagles had to trade two starting players and a draft pick to the Rams to get the quarterback, no one in Philadelphia complained. Van Brocklin's on-field leadership and great passing arm carried the Eagles to an improved 7–5 mark in 1959.

In 1960, the Eagles peaked. After losing two linebackers to injuries late in the season, Philadelphia reinstated Bednarik's 60-minute workload. The Eagles and their veteran iron man rolled to a 10–2 record and won the Eastern Division title. Philadelphia then faced off against legendary coach Vince Lombardi and the Green Bay Packers in the NFL Championship Game.

The game was a hard-fought contest between two of the

NORM VAN BROCKLIN LED PHILADELPHIA TO A CHAMPIONSHIP IN HIS FINAL SEASON

Chuck Bednarik

CENTER, LINEBACKER / EAGLES SEASONS: 1949–62 / HEIGHT: 6-FOOT-3 / WEIGHT: 233 POUNDS

Chuck Bednarik was a true iron man of the NFL. Playing center on offense and middle linebacker on defense, the hard-nosed star was even on the field for special-teams plays. On offense, he was a bulldozing blocker, and as a linebacker, he was a feared hitter. Bednarik is best known for two remarkable plays, both of which occurred during the 1960 season. The first happened in a game against the New York Giants. As New York tried to mount a fourth-quarter comeback in a 17–10 game, the "60-Minute Man" hit Giants star running back Frank Gifford hard enough to both cause a game-ending fumble and knock Gifford out cold. Then, late in the 1960 NFL Championship Game, with Philadelphia leading 17–13, Green Bay Packers halfback Jim Taylor was streaking toward the end zone before the 35-year-old Bednarik ran him down and wrestled him to the ground as the clock expired. During and after his football career, Bednarik also sold concrete, prompting a local sportswriter to dub him "Concrete Charlie," stating that he was "as hard as the concrete he sells."

toughest teams in football. The Eagles trailed 13–10 in the fourth quarter before The Dutchman—as he had done all season—engineered a game-winning drive. "He was like a coach on the field," Bednarik said of Van Brocklin, who was named the NFL's Most Valuable Player (MVP) of the 1960 season.

Philadelphia fans savored the 1960 season, and it was a good thing, because it would take 18 years and 6 different coaches before the Eagles would make the playoffs again. Still, the team put on some good shows in the 1960s, including a remarkable 1961 season by new quarterback Sonny Jurgensen, who passed for 3,723 yards and 32 touchdowns. Fans also saw an NFL record-setting performance (2,306 all-purpose yards) by running back Timmy Brown in 1962. The next year, the Eagles were purchased by Washington, D.C., businessman Jerry Wolman, who, despite numerous trades, could not field a winning team in Philadelphia.

he Eagles were sold again in 1969 to a millionaire trucking executive named Leonard Tose, who reportedly paid $16.1 million for the Philadelphia franchise—a record price for the purchase of any professional sports team at the time. Two years later, he moved the team from Franklin Field to Veterans Stadium, which the Eagles would call home for the next three decades.

It was more of the same for the Eagles in the early 1970s, as the team consistently failed to assemble a winning record. In 1972, receiver Harold Jackson led the league in both receptions (62) and receiving yards (1,048). The next year, a towering young receiver named Harold Carmichael emerged to lead the league with 67 catches. Despite such strong performances, the Eagles were a team that just couldn't fly.

Things finally changed for the better in 1976, when Dick Vermeil was named head coach. Vermeil believed that the only path to greatness was through hard work, and "Coach V" worked tirelessly to turn the Eagles around, often sleeping in his office instead of at home. "I don't want to put our other coaches down," Tose said as he introduced Vermeil. "But I'm telling you that this time the Philadelphia fans are getting the real thing—a great coach."

In 1978, Coach Vermeil's efforts paid off, as the Eagles went 9–7 and returned to the playoffs for the

Fly, Eagles, Fly!

When Jerry Wolman owned the Eagles during the 1960s, his daughter frequently accompanied him to games. After hearing the rival Washington Redskins fans belt out their team's war chant, she implored her father to let her create a song that would rally Eagles fans and energize their stadium for home games. The resulting song was "Fly, Eagles, Fly!" The fight song was a hit with fans, but after a few years, its popularity waned. It wasn't until Jeffrey Lurie bought the Eagles in 1994 that the song was brought back to the stadium to be blasted through the stadium loudspeakers during Eagles games once again. Eagles fans latched on to the old song and today sing it after every touchdown and sometimes for no apparent reason at all. The song has even been heard at Philadelphia Phillies baseball, Flyers hockey, 76ers basketball, and Soul arena football games. Fans sometimes take liberties with the words to include their current opponent in the song. After more than five decades, "Fly, Eagles, Fly!" remains one of the most popular team anthems in the NFL.

MUSICALLY INCLINED EAGLES FANS BELT OUT THE TEAM SONG BEFORE GAMES

BILL BERGEY PATROLLED THE MIDDLE OF THE EAGLES' DEFENSE IN THE 1970s

RON JAWORSKI AND DICK VERMEIL STRATEGIZED TO GET TO THE SUPER BOWL

first of two straight seasons. Although fans were disappointed when the team suffered playoff defeats both times, they were sure the Eagles could win it all if Coach Vermeil could get his team to improve one more notch.

hanks to a strong offensive showing in 1980 by Carmichael, quarterback Ron Jaworski, and veteran running back Wilbert Montgomery, Philadelphia surged to the top of the National Football Conference's (NFC) East Division. "Philly" fans then cheered as the Eagles flew by the Minnesota Vikings and Dallas Cowboys to land in Super Bowl XV, where they faced the Oakland Raiders.

Although the Raiders topped the Eagles 27–10 on Super Bowl Sunday at the Louisiana Superdome, the Eagles held their heads high. "Four years ago, this team was a doormat," said Jaworski, who was named the NFL's Player of the Year. "Now we're Super Bowl material. You know how satisfying that is?"

Coach Vermeil led the Eagles back to the playoffs in 1981 but then resigned just nine victories short of surpassing Greasy Neale as the winningest coach in franchise history. In seven seasons, Coach V had guided the Eagles to 57 victories, 7 playoff games, 1 Super Bowl, . . . and newfound respectability.

The Santa Incident

Eagles fans are notoriously vocal and can sometimes be a bit out of control, as they displayed during halftime of a 1968 game when, in a famous incident, they pelted Santa Claus with snowballs. At the time, the Eagles franchise was becoming a perennial loser, in part because of moves made by team owner Jerry Wolman and coach and general manager Joe Kuharich. On December 15, when the Minnesota Vikings came to town, Eagles fans were supposed to be treated to a halftime Christmas pageant, complete with music and a decorated float. Due to a large snowfall, the pageant fell through, and the team instead hired 19-year-old Frank Olivo, a fan who had worn a Santa Claus costume to the game, to do an improvised run around the field. The disgruntled fans saw him as a representative of the team's poor management and used the plentiful snow to take out their frustrations on the poor volunteer with a shower of snowballs. Olivo escaped unharmed and without a grudge. He later said, "I'm a Philadelphia fan. I knew what was what. I thought it was funny."

WHO WOULD THROW SNOWBALLS AT SANTA? EAGLES FANS, THAT'S WHO!

REGGIE WHITE (#92) PREACHED TOUGH DEFENSE TO HIS TEAMMATES

The Minister and the Scrambler

Without Coach Vermeil, the Eagles stumbled badly over the next several years. Philadelphia clearly needed something big, and in 1985, it got it in the form of 6-foot-5 and 300-pound defensive end Reggie White. White was an ordained Baptist minister who had earned the nickname "The Minister of Defense" while dominating the United States Football League as part of a team called the Memphis Showboats. Once signed by the Eagles, the enormous end made 13 quarterback sacks to earn 1985 NFL Defensive Rookie of the Year honors.

Unfortunately for Eagles opponents, that was just the beginning. Playing alongside defensive linemen Greg Brown and Ken Clarke, White spearheaded an increasingly frightening pass rush. In 1986, he added 18 sacks to Brown and Clarke's combined 17. By the time he ended his Philadelphia career in 1992, White would be the only player in NFL history to have more sacks (124) than games played (121).

IF HE COULDN'T FIND AN OPEN RECEIVER, RANDALL CUNNINGHAM COULD RUN

Harold Carmichael

WIDE RECEIVER / EAGLES SEASONS: 1971–83 / HEIGHT: 6-FOOT-8 / WEIGHT: 225 POUNDS

A quarterback loves a big target. That's especially true when his team is in the red zone (inside the 20-yard line) and ready to score. Harold Carmichael was a full 6-foot-8 when he lined up for the Eagles. His size alone created matchup problems for defenses, who would try to double-team him with two cornerbacks who were frequently almost a foot shorter than he was. Eagles quarterbacks such as Ron Jaworski needed only to throw the ball up high, and Carmichael would go up and snatch it out of the air above the defenders' heads. But Carmichael was more than just a tall body. He was a fast runner with rare leaping ability and remarkable durability. Between 1972 and 1983, he played in 162 straight games for the Eagles. Carmichael appeared in four Pro Bowls and still holds Eagles franchise records for touchdowns (79), receiving yards (8,978), and receptions (589). "He was the first big receiver in the NFL," said Alva Tabor, who coached Carmichael at Louisiana's Southern University and A&M College. "Harold actually changed the game."

AS A ROOKIE, TIGHT END KEITH JACKSON LED THE EAGLES IN CATCHES

H oping to build a mighty defense around White, the Eagles hired former Chicago Bears defensive coordinator Buddy Ryan as head coach in 1986. Coach Ryan began installing the same defensive game plan that he had used to propel the 1985 Bears to a Super Bowl victory. And while he was thrilled with some of the team's defensive talent, Ryan was perhaps most impressed with young quarterback Randall Cunningham.

During his college career at the University of Nevada, Las Vegas, the tall and lanky Cunningham had proven to be a sensational athlete, able to sprint like a wide receiver or to launch the ball more than 70 yards down the field. Finally given the chance to start in 1987, Cunningham made good on the opportunity by throwing 23 touchdown passes. After the season, as Cunningham recalled, "Buddy came to me and said, 'It's your offense. If it doesn't work, it's going to be your fault.' I don't mind that at all."

Philadelphia fans didn't mind, either, as Cunningham and the Eagles began to soar. In 1988, he and rookie tight end Keith Jackson led the team to a 10–6 record and a playoff berth. Unfortunately, the Eagles lost to the Bears 20–12 in a bizarre, mist-shrouded playoff game dubbed "The Fog Bowl." The next year, the defense notched a team-record 62 sacks as the Eagles stormed to an 11–5 mark and another playoff berth. But the strong offense of the Los Angeles Rams was too much for the Eagles, as Los Angeles dealt Philadelphia a 21–7 defeat.

In 1990, Cunningham enjoyed the best season of his Philadelphia career, throwing

PLAYERS COULD BARELY SEE THE ACTION THROUGH THE HAZE OF THE "FOG BOWL"

A Super Bowl at Last

After three straight years of making it to the NFC Championship Game but coming up short, the Eagles finally earned their way into the big game after the 2004 season. Facing the reigning Super Bowl champion New England Patriots, the Eagles were the obvious underdogs in the matchup. The Eagles got a big boost before the game, though, when star receiver Terrell Owens—who was recovering from a fractured leg—was pronounced healthy enough to play. The Eagles struck first on Super Bowl Sunday when Donovan McNabb connected with tight end L. J. Smith in the second quarter for a touchdown. At the end of three quarters, the game was knotted at 14–14. In the final quarter, the Patriots dominated the Eagles to jump ahead 24–14. Owens did his part, leading the team with 122 receiving yards, but the Eagles could not close the gap, losing 24–21. Although they lost, the Eagles had put up more of a fight than many experts predicted. "We just didn't make enough plays to get the victory," said Philadelphia cornerback Lito Sheppard, "and they didn't make that many mistakes."

L. J. SMITH CELEBRATED IN THE END ZONE AT JACKSONVILLE'S ALLTEL STADIUM

AT 6-FOOT-2 AND 292 POUNDS, JEROME BROWN BULKED UP THE DEFENSIVE LINE

for 3,466 yards and running for an incredible 942 more. Unfortunately, despite his efforts and those of White, Jackson, and defensive tackle Jerome Brown, the Eagles lost in the first round of the playoffs for a third straight year. Coach Ryan was then fired, and White and Jackson soon left town. It was time for the Eagles to rebuild.

The mid-1990s were mediocre seasons in Philadelphia. The Eagles made the postseason in 1995 with a 10–6 record under head coach Ray Rhodes and even blew out the Detroit Lions, 58–37, in a playoff game. But the eventual Super Bowl champion Dallas Cowboys crushed them a week later, 30–11. New standouts such as fiery running back Ricky Watters stepped forward, but they couldn't stop the downward slide. By 1998, the once-mighty Eagles were just 3–13.

ANDY REID'S EAGLES SQUADS WON SEVEN DIVISION CHAMPIONSHIPS

Reid Takes the Reins

The hiring of former Green Bay Packers assistant coach Andy Reid in 1999 sparked a resurgence in Philly. The Eagles improved their record by just two games during Reid's first season but soared to an 11–5 mark in 2000.

The driving force behind this improvement was second-year quarterback Donovan McNabb. Burly and athletic, McNabb drew comparisons to Randall Cunningham as he threw for 3,365 yards and rushed for 629 in 2000. McNabb had been booed by fans when he was drafted by the Eagles, but in less than two years he'd emerged as a Pro Bowl talent. "Donovan's a sharp kid," Coach Reid said, "and I know he'll turn into a top-notch NFL quarterback."

Philadelphia became tougher on the other side of the ball as well in 2000. Pass-rushing expert Hugh Douglas, along with cover corner Troy Vincent and bone-crunching safety Brian Dawkins, led an aggressive defense that stifled the Tampa Bay Buccaneers in a 21–3 playoff victory—Philadelphia's first postseason win in five years.

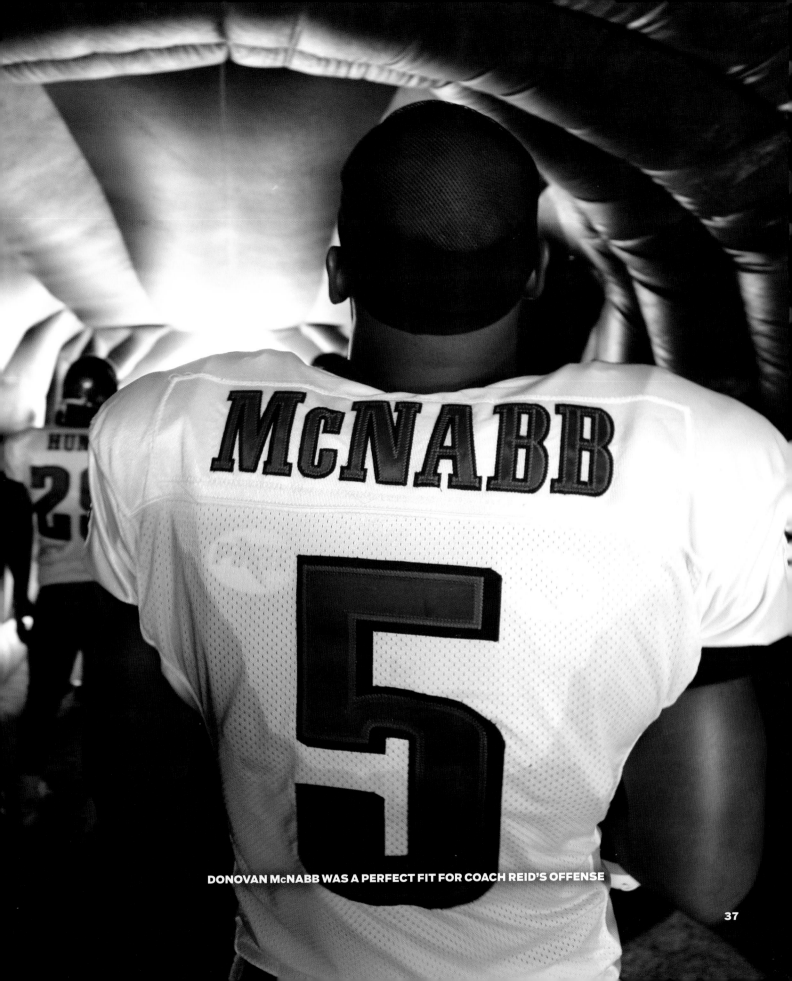

DONOVAN McNABB WAS A PERFECT FIT FOR COACH REID'S OFFENSE

Reggie White

DEFENSIVE END / EAGLES SEASONS: 1985–92 / HEIGHT: 6-FOOT-5 / WEIGHT: 300 POUNDS

Dubbed "The Minister of Defense" during his senior season at the University of Tennessee after becoming an ordained minister at age 17, White brought a rare passion for stopping opposing offenses with him to the NFL. He gave Eagles fans a glimpse of the future in 1985 as he tallied 2.5 sacks in his very first game and 13 sacks in only 13 games his first season, earning Defensive Rookie of the Year honors. Year after year, he put up double-digit sack totals, and he was selected to 13 straight Pro Bowls. In 1987, White put together one of the best years by any defensive lineman in history by collecting 21 sacks during a strike-shortened season that lasted just 12 games. Although White was dominant at disrupting offenses and harrying quarterbacks on the field, he was also considered a valuable leader and mentor to his teammates. After White passed away in 2004, former NFL commissioner Paul Tagliabue summarized his legacy by saying, "Reggie White was a gentle warrior who will be remembered as one of the greatest defensive players in NFL history."

The still-improving Eagles advanced to the NFC Championship Game each of the following two seasons but came up short of the Super Bowl both times. The 2002 loss to Tampa Bay was particularly disappointing to Philly fans, as it was the last game ever played in Veterans Stadium, the team's home since 1971.

Fortunately, the Eagles adjusted well to their new home—Lincoln Financial Field—and in 2003 posted an NFC-best 12–4 record. Helping McNabb that year was versatile halfback Brian Westbrook, who led the team in rushing and receiving touchdowns, and was dangerous as a return man on both punts and kickoffs. Despite the change in location and emergence of Westbrook, the 2003 season ended the same way. After Philadelphia

THE EAGLES MADE LINCOLN FINANCIAL FIELD AN INTIMIDATING PLACE TO PLAY

defeated Green Bay in dramatic fashion to reach the NFC Championship Game, it once again came up just short of the Super Bowl, losing to the Carolina Panthers, 14–3.

To get over the hump, Philadelphia bolstered its roster in the off-season. The club brought back former Eagles defensive end Hugh Douglas and linebacker Jeremiah Trotter. It also added Jevon Kearse, a defensive end so fast and relentless in his pursuit of quarterbacks that he was nicknamed "The Freak." While Kearse's signing was worthy of headlines, it was overshadowed by the acquisition of Terrell Owens, a big, fast receiver known for both exceptional talent and an over-the-top ego.

The revamped Eagles came out swinging in 2004. Owens amassed 14 touchdowns and 1,200 receiving yards, Westbrook became even more dangerous out of the backfield, and Philadelphia streaked to a franchise-best 13–3 record. The Eagles overwhelmed the Minnesota Vikings and Atlanta Falcons in the playoffs to reach the Super Bowl for the first time since 1980. There they faced the reigning champion New England Patriots. The Eagles matched the Patriots point for point for the first three quarters and outplayed New England in many ways, but four Philadelphia turnovers were too much to overcome in the end. New England celebrated a 24–21 win, while the Eagles went home empty-handed.

The disappointment of that loss seemed to stick with the Eagles as they plummeted to 6–10 in 2005. Part of the problem was that McNabb suffered nagging injuries and Owens refused to play during a contract holdout. The Eagles jettisoned Owens the following year, and McNabb was once again hampered by injuries. The 2006 Eagles still performed well enough to reach the playoffs. But after a three-point win

A Second Chance

In 2001, the Atlanta Falcons selected quarterback Michael Vick with the first pick in the NFL Draft. A phenomenal athlete, Vick could outrun most defenders and throw the pigskin more than 70 yards. His freakish talents made him a fan favorite around the league, but his undisciplined style of play limited his effectiveness. Meanwhile, his off-field decisions were even more troubling. In 2007, Vick was found guilty of running a brutal dogfighting operation and sentenced to 23 months in prison. Many disgusted fans assumed that was the end of Vick's football career. However, when his prison sentence ended, Vick wanted another chance. While most teams were unwilling to sign the gifted but controversial quarterback, Philadelphia rolled the dice and added Vick to its roster in 2009. He played sparingly that season, but when starting quarterback Kevin Kolb was injured in early 2010, Vick stepped in and had the best season of his career, completing nearly 63 percent of his passes for 3,018 yards and 21 touchdowns while rushing for 9 more scores. "I've come a long way," Vick said after the season. "I hate to relive the past, ... but everything happens for a reason."

MICHAEL VICK LEFT SCANDAL BEHIND AND FOUND A NEW HOME IN PHILADELPHIA

CORNERBACK ASANTE SAMUEL LED THE NFL WITH 9 INTERCEPTIONS IN 2009

over the division rival Giants, Philly suffered a three-point defeat at the hands of the New Orleans Saints.

The next season was the best of Westbrook's career, and defensive end Trent Cole proved to be a nightmare for runners and quarterbacks alike, but the Eagles would not reach the postseason again until 2008, when they sneaked in after a season with just nine wins and one tie. Despite its modest record, Philadelphia rallied to defeat the Vikings and Giants to reach the NFC Championship Game for the fifth time in eight years. The Eagles held a 25–24 lead over the Arizona Cardinals late in the fourth quarter, but a final scoring drive by the Cardinals squashed Philly's hopes of a return to the Super Bowl.

By 2009, the Eagles had grown weary of their near misses. That off-season, they made the controversial decision to sign quarterback Michael Vick, who had spent the previous two years in prison and had upset many fans because of his involvement in the cruel blood sport of dogfighting. Vick played sparingly while McNabb led the Eagles to a solid 11–5 record. Unfortunately, a first-round loss in the playoffs marked the end of McNabb's tenure in Philadelphia.

Vick shocked the NFL the following year by enjoying the most complete season of his career. Vick had always been a great athlete with swift feet and a cannon of an arm, but in 2010 he demonstrated poise and leadership that he'd never shown before. He carried the Eagles to a 10–6 season and easily won the NFL's Comeback Player of the Year award. Philadelphia lost another round-one playoff game, but its future continued to look bright.

That future seemed to brighten further when the Eagles added several talented defensive players in the 2011 off-season, including shutdown corner Nnamdi Asomugha. On the other side of the ball,

Randall Cunningham

QUARTERBACK / EAGLES SEASONS: 1985—95 / HEIGHT: 6-FOOT-4 / WEIGHT: 212 POUNDS

What does a defense do when the opposing quarterback isn't just a pocket passer, or a traditional scrambler, but a real threat to run the ball for a touchdown from any distance? That's what defensive coordinators had to figure out when they faced the Eagles and Randall Cunningham. A superb all-around athlete, Cunningham had a strong arm, great speed, and the elusive moves of a star running back. After replacing Ron Jaworski as the starting quarterback in 1987, he gave Eagles fans a show they'd never forget. For the next four seasons, Cunningham was not only a prolific passer but also the leading rusher on the team. In one 1989 game, he displayed yet another aspect of his athleticism with a surprise 91-yard punt that helped the Eagles beat the New York Giants in a key game. While the NFL has seen great passers, marvelous scramblers, and even some strong runners at the quarterback position, perhaps no one put them together as well as Cunningham. His style of play paved the way for future fleet-footed quarterbacks such as Donovan McNabb and Michael Vick to be more than just pocket passers.

DEFENSE HAS LONG BEEN A CORNERSTONE OF THE EAGLES' SUCCESS

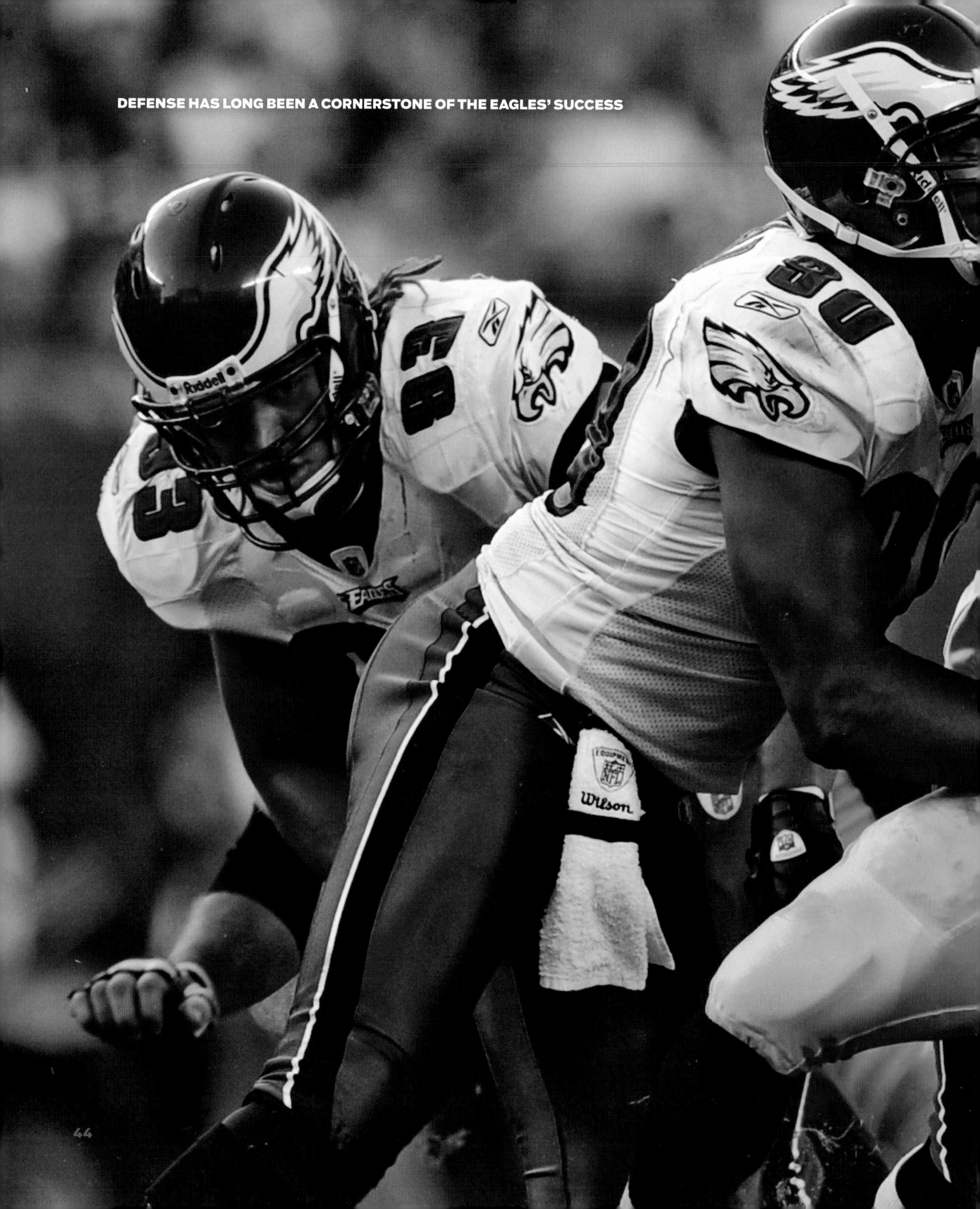

AS BOTH A RECEIVER AND A RETURN SPECIALIST, DeSEAN JACKSON WAS A GAME-CHANGER

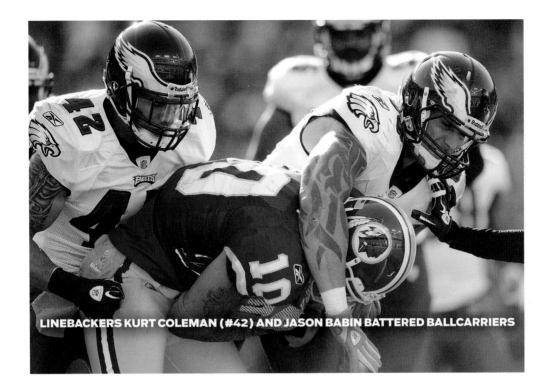

LINEBACKERS KURT COLEMAN (#42) AND JASON BABIN BATTERED BALLCARRIERS

two lightning-quick scoring threats—running back LeSean McCoy and receiver DeSean Jackson—were coming into their prime. Unfortunately, great individual talent didn't translate to great team success, and the Eagles struggled early in 2011. They seemed to find the right chemistry late in the season, finishing with a four-game winning streak, but it was too little too late. Philadelphia missed the playoffs with a middling 8–8 mark.

Hoping to shore up their defense, the Eagles traded up in the 2012 Draft to take tackle Fletcher Cox with the 12th overall pick. Cox did his share throughout the season, leading all Philly defensive linemen with 85 tackles and making NFL Draft guru Mel Kiper's All-Rookie team. "Cox has a chance to become a Pro Bowl–level interior lineman," Kiper said.

Unfortunately, few other Eagles players seemed to be at that level. After opening the season 3–1, the Eagles had their wings clipped, going 0-for-8 in October and November. They finally notched win number four—a two-point triumph over Tampa Bay on December 9—but dropped their final three contests to finish 4–12. Coach Reid was fired and replaced by the University of Oregon's Chip Kelly, a dynamic personality with no previous experience at the pro level.

The historic city of Philadelphia has long been a site of stubborn resilience, and over the course of eight decades, the Philadelphia Eagles have embodied that attitude on the gridiron. From the helmetless Bill Hewitt and Chuck "60-Minute Man" Bednarik, to The Minister of Defense and the hard-nosed Donovan McNabb, Philadelphia players have always been tough, and their fans always demanding. Today's young and talented Eagles hope to add to that legacy and soon soar above the competition.